T R I S T A N
AND ISOLDA

Opera in Three Acts

By

RICHARD WAGNER

Vocal Score by
RICHARD KLEINMICHEL

English Version by
HENRY GRAFTON CHAPMAN

With an Essay on the
Story of the Opera by
H. E. KREHBIEL

Night-affirming Tristan, followed by Meistersinger, which affirms day.

German Romantic theory that night is the really meaningful time: Novalis (Hymns to the Night) Schopenhauer

Ed. 619

G. SCHIRMER, Inc.
Distributed by
Hal Leonard Publishing Corporation
7777 West Bluemound Road P.O. Box 13819 Milwaukee, WI 53213

TRISTAN AND ISOLDA
DRAMA IN THREE ACTS

CHARACTERS

TRISTAN	*Tenor*	MELOT	*Tenor*
KING MARK	*Bass*	BRANGÆNA	*Soprano*
ISOLDA	*Soprano*	A SHEPHERD	*Tenor*
KURVENAL	*Baritone*	A HELMSMAN	*Baritone*

SAILORS, KNIGHTS AND ATTENDANTS

SCENE OF ACTION

Act I. At sea on the deck of Tristan's ship, on the voyage from Ireland to Cornwall.

Act II. King Mark's castle in Cornwall.

Act III. Tristan's castle in Brittany.

. .

The drama was first performed at Munich on June 10, 1865
with the following cast:

TRISTAN	*Herr Schnorr von Carolsfeld*
ISOLDE	*Frau Schnorr von Carolsfeld*
KÖNIG MARKE	*Herr Zottmayer*
KURWENAL	*Herr Mitterwurzer*
MELOT	*Herr Heinrich*
BRANGÄNE	*Frl. Deinet*
EIN HIRT	*Herr Simons*
EIN STEUERMANN	*Herr Hartmann*

TRISTAN AND ISOLDA

"A VASSAL is sent to woo a beauteous princess for his lord. While he is bringing her home the two, by accident, drink a love-potion, and ever thereafter their hearts are fettered together. In the mid-day of delirious joy, in the midnight of deepest woe, and through all the emotional hours between, their thoughts are only of each other, for each other. Meanwhile the princess has become the vassal's queen. Then the wicked love of the pair is discovered, and the knight is obliged to seek safety in a foreign land. There (strange note this to our ears) he marries another princess, whose name is like that of his love, save for the addition 'With the White Hand;' but when wounded unto death he sends across the water for her who is still his true love, that she come and be his healer. The ship which is sent to bring her is to bear white sails on its return if successful in the mission; black, if not. Day after day the knight waits for the coming of his love, while the lamp of his life burns lower and lower. At length the sails of the ship appear on the distant horizon. The knight is now himself too weak to look. 'White or black?' he asks of his wife. 'Black,' replies she, jealousy prompting the falsehood; and the knight's heart-strings snap in twain just as his love steps over the threshold of the chamber. Oh, the pity of it! for with the lady is her lord, who, having learned the story of the fateful potion, has come to unite the lovers. Then the queen, too, dies, and the remorseful king buries the lovers in a common grave, from whose caressing sod spring a rose-bush and a vine and intertwine so curiously that none may separate them."* Thus, in simplest outline, runs the legend which Wagner has given dramatic form in his "Tristan und Isolde." It was long in the poet-composer's mind before it took shape. Wagner was an omnivorous reader; but it was during the period of his activity as operatic conductor in Dresden, from 1843 to 1849, that he gave particular attention to the study of old Germanic legends. How these studies bore fruit in "Lohengrin," "Tannhäuser," "Wieland der Schmiedt" (which remained a sketch), "Siegfried's Tod" (which grew into "Götterdämmerung" and eventually into the Nibelung trilogy), and "Parsifal," the world knows. The legend of Tristram (or Tristan, to adopt the German appellation) is of vast antiquity; its origin is lost in the mists of early civilizations, like those of its companions which tell of Siegfried and Parsifal, with which it has elements in common and which had loving communion in Wagner's mind. As we know it, the tale of Tristan is Keltic, and it is at least remotely possible that the original Aryan root first blossomed in modern

* "Studies in the Wagnerian Drama," by H. E. Krehbiel.

literary form in Wales. This was the fond belief of Sir Walter Scott, who in 1804 edited a metrical version attributed to Thomas the Rhymer, who was supposed to have been a poet of the fourteenth century. This branch of curious and interesting inquiry does not necessarily call for attention here, however, since the source followed by Wagner is sufficiently obvious. Enough that the singular charm of the tale "which half a millennium of poets have celebrated as the High Song of Love, the Canticle of all Canticles which hymn the universal passion" (*op. cit.*), is alike familiar to English and German literature. It has been told by Sir Thomas Malory, Lord Tennyson, Matthew Arnold, and Algernon Swinburne, each of whom has placed the stamp of his peculiar genius upon it. Long ago the love-song was sung by the French trouvères, and after them by the German Minnesinger. The most famous mediæval version is the German epic of Gottfried von Strassburg, a translation of which into the modern language by Hermann Kurtz was published in 1844. This, it may safely be assumed, fell under the eye of Wagner while he was delving in the legendary lore of his people in the Dresden period. Gottfried left the story unfinished, but two poets of his century, the thirteenth, were his continuators. Following these—Ulrich von Türnheim and Heinrich von Freiberg—Kurtz wrote the dénouement indicated in our outline, namely, the life of the hero in Brittany with Isolde of the White Hand, and his death as the immediate result of the falsehood about the sails. While Wagner was sketching his drama in 1855 an edition of Gottfried's epic appeared under the editorship of Karl Simrock. It offered nothing new in the reading of the text, but there were some ingenious allusions in the preface which seem to have provided Wagner with some of the pictures and symbolism with which the second act of his tragedy is rife. These were the dawn of day during the lovers' meeting (of which Shakespeare made such exquisite use in "Romeo and Juliet"), and the fateful result of the extinguishment of the torch, which has a prototype in the ancient legend of Hero and Leander. The incident of the sails belongs to Greek story—the legend of Ægeus and Theseus. Wagner evidently intended to employ the incident in a changed form, turning the black sails into a black flag, for, writing to Liszt late in 1854, he said: "As I have never in my life enjoyed the true felicity of love, I shall erect to this most beautiful of my dreams [he refers to the Siegfried drama] a monument in which, from beginning to end, this love shall find fullest gratification. I have sketched in my head a 'Tristan und Isolde,' the simplest of musical conceptions, but full-blooded; with the 'black flag' which waves at the end I shall then cover myself—to die." Other significant departures from the old legend made by Wagner, obviously for the purpose of intensifying and ennobling the character and passion of the fabled lovers, are the omission of the element of accident in the drinking of the potion, and the second Isolde. Concerning the first of these I have spoken at considerable length in the book quoted at the beginning of this preface, and, since it is a matter that goes deep into the ethics of the drama, I may, perhaps, be pardoned for repeating some of my words: "The versions of Gottfried von Strassburg, Matthew Arnold, Swinburne, Tennyson and Wagner present three points of view from which the love of the tragic pair must be studied. With the first three the drinking is purely accidental, and the passion which leads to the destruction of the lovers is something for which they are in no wise responsible. With Tennyson there is no philtre, and the passion is all guilty. With Wagner the love exists before the dreadful drinking, and the potion is less a maker of uncontrollable passion than a drink which causes the lovers to forget duty, honor and the respect due to the laws of society. It is a favorite idea of Wagner's that the hero of tragedy should be a type of humanity freed from all bonds of conventionality. It is unquestionable, in my mind, that in his scheme we are to accept the love-potion as merely the agency with which Wagner struck from his hero the shackles of convention. Unquestionably, as Bayard Taylor argued, the love-draught is the Fate of the Tristan drama, and this brings into notice the significance of Wagner's chief variation. It is an old theory, too often overlooked now, that there must be at least a taint of guilt in the conduct of a tragic hero in order that the feeling of pity excited by his sufferings may not overcome the idea of justice in the catastrophe. This theory was plainly an outgrowth of the deep religious purpose of the Greek tragedy. Wagner puts antecedent and conscious guilt at the door of both of his heroic characters. They love before the philtre, and do not pay the reverence to the passion which, in the highest conception, it commands. Tristan is carried away by love of power and glory before men, and himself suggests and compels by his threats Marke's marriage, which is a crime against the love which he bears Isolde and she bears him. There is guilt enough in Isolde's determination and effort to commit murder and suicide. Thus Wagner presents us the idea of Fate in the latest and highest aspect that it assumed in the minds of the Greek poets, and he arouses our pity and our horror, not only by the sufferings of the principals, but also by making an innocent and amiable prompting to underlie the action which brings down the catastrophe. It is Brangäne's love for her mistress that persuades her to shield her from the crime of murder and protect her life. From whatever point of view the question is treated, it seems to me that Wagner's variation is an improvement on the old legends, and that the objection, which German critics have urged, that the love of the pair is merely a chemical product, and so outside of human sympathy, falls to the ground."

The letter to Liszt from which a brief quotation has been made indicates that "Tristan und Isolde" had its inception in Wagner's mind in the fall of 1854. He was then living in Zurich, and it was three years before he began the execution of his plan. It was not to be a monument to a dream of felicity never experienced, or to his despair at ever seeing the completion of his "Siegfried" drama (which had advanced to the second act when it was laid aside), but the tribute to a consuming passion for the wife of a benefactor, whose generosity provided him with an idyllic home at Triebschen on the shores of Lake Lucerne. Love for Mathilde Wesendonck was the inspiration of both book and score, and it speaks tumultuously and with unexampled eloquence in the love music of the second act. Not until Wagner's letters to the lady were published, long years after both were dead, were all the facts in the case known. Frau Wesendonck was the author of the "Fünf Gedichte" which owe their preservation to the music to which Wagner wedded them. Two of the songs, "Im Treibhaus" and "Träume," when published were described as "Studies for Tristan und Isolde," and the latter at least may be set down as having, in a special sense, an autobiographical value. Four of the five were composed in the winter of 1857–58; "Im Treibhaus" on May 1, 1858. The theme of "Träume" was the germ of the love music of the second act of the tragedy, that of "Im Treibhaus" of the prelude to the third act. The prose scenario of the drama was written in August, 1857, finding its completion on the 20th day of that month, and the poem was practically finished within a month thereafter, that is to say, by September 18th. The pencil sketches of the music, all painstakingly and lovingly written over in ink by Frau Wesendonck, to whom they were presented by the composer, bear dates as follows: Act I, October 1, 1857, to New Year's eve; Act II, May 4 to July 1, 1858; Act III, April 9 to July 16, 1859. So much for what may be called the inner, or psychological, history of the work; its outward story is more prosaic. In May, 1857, after Wagner had been eight years an exile from his native land, he received an invitation from Dom Pedro, Emperor of Brazil, to write an opera for Rio de Janeiro, come to the Brazilian capital, and conduct its first performances. It does not appear that Wagner ever seriously contemplated accepting the invitation, but it set him to thinking, and may have been the jolt which turned his mind again to the project which he had announced to Liszt two and a half years previously. Years had passed since he had begun work on "Der Ring des Nibelungen," and that stupendous enterprise held out little promise of fruition in the way of publication, and less of performance and royalties. At any rate he formulated a plan to write the opera in German, have it translated into Italian, dedicate the score to the Emperor of Brazil, and permit the performance in Rio de Janeiro, utilizing the occasion, if possible, to secure a performance of "Tannhäuser" beforehand. Meanwhile he would have the opera produced in its original tongue at Strassburg, then a French city conveniently near the German border, with Niemann in the titular rôle and an orchestra from Karlsruhe, or some other German city containing an opera-house. Of course, he communicated the plan to Liszt at once, and equally of course, Liszt approved the project heartily, though he was greatly amazed at the intelligence which he had from another source that Wagner intended to write the music with an eye to a performance in Italian. "How in the name of all the gods are you going to make of it an opera for Italian singers, as B. tells me you are? Well, since the incredible and impossible have become your elements, perhaps you will achieve this too;" and he promised to go to Strassburg with the Wagnerian coterie as a guard of honor for the composer. Nothing came of either plan, as we shall see, but Wagner, under a vastly different stimulus, wrote the opera, doing much of the work in Venice, whither he went that he might have quiet and work undisturbedly. He had carried on fruitless negotiations with Breitkopf & Härtel for the publication of his "Ring des Nibelungen," but the new opera seemed like a more practical proposition to the publishers, and they agreed to take the score for the equivalent of $800, which sum they were to pay him on the receipt of the first act. When the project of the German performance was revived, Eduard Devrient, director of the Grand Ducal Theatre at Karlsruhe, persuaded the composer to give up Strassburg in favor of his city, which, in Schnorr von Carolsfeld and his wife, contained two artists in every way adapted to create the hero and heroine of the tragedy. Wagner wanted to supervise the production, however, and this was impossible so long as the decree of banishment for his political offences in Saxony was still in force. The Grand Duke of Baden appealed in his behalf to the King of Saxony, but all in vain; and in the fall of 1859 Wagner went to Paris, cherishing a dream of a performance there with German singers. This project, too, failed, and Wagner found that all that was left for him to do in the way of propagandism for his art was to give some concerts in Paris and Brussels, and finally, in 1861, to give the performances at the Grand Opera which resulted in one of the most famous and disgraceful scandals in musical history, a scandal compared with which the *guerre des buffons* and the combat of Gluckists and Piccinnists in the same city a century earlier was as child's play. Again began the search for a city in which "Tristan" might have its first hearing. Weimar, Prague, and Hanover were canvassed, and in the end Wagner turned to Vienna. Two years had elapsed since the score had been completed, and Wagner was consumed with desire to hear it, and as positive as he was of his own existence (so he writes to Ferdinand Praeger) that it was without an equal in all the world's library of music. To Vienna he now went, arriving there in May, 1861. He did not get his heart's desire, but he heard his "Lohengrin" for the first time—"Lohengrin," which had been composed thirteen years before. As for "Tristan," it was accepted for performance at the Court Opera after some delay, and rehearsals begun; but after fifty-four of these, between November, 1862, and March, 1863, it was abandoned as "impossible." The next year saw the turning-point in Wagner's career: Ludwig of Bavaria became his friend and patron. Wagner went to Munich, and within a few months it was arranged that "Tristan und Isolde" should be performed at the Royal Court Theatre. On April 18, 1865, a public invitation went out from Wagner through the columns of a Viennese newspaper to his friends to attend the projected performance. Schnorr von Carolsfeld and his wife were brought from Dresden, whither they had gone from Karlsruhe, to create the principal characters; the composer's friends, official and unofficial, foregathered in large numbers, and after several trying postponements the first performance took place under the direction of Hans von Bülow, who had made the pianoforte score of the work, on June 10, 1865. The principal parts were distributed as follows: *Tristan*, Ludwig Schnorr von Carolsfeld; *Kurwenal*, Mitterwurzer; *Melot*, Heinrich; *König Marke*, Zottmayer; *Isolde*, Frau Schnorr von Carolsfeld; *Brangäne*, Fräulein Deinet. Twenty-one-and-a-half years later the tragedy reached New York, when it had its performance on December 1, 1886, with Albert Niemann, whom the composer had chosen to be the original creator of his hero in Strassburg, as *Tristan*, and Anton Seidl, the composer's pupil and apostle, in the conductor's chair. The parts were distributed as follows: *Isolde*, Fräulein Lilli Lehmann; *Brangäne*, Marianne Brandt; *Tristan*, Albert Niemann; *Kurwenal*, Adolf Robinson; *König Marke*, Emil Fischer; *Melot*, Rudolph von Milde; *Ein Hirt*, Otto Kemlitz; *Ein Steuermann*, Emil Saenger; *Ein Seemann*, Max Alvary.

Act I. The scene is laid on board of a ship which is within a short sail of Cornwall. Thither *Tristan* is bearing *Isolde*, daughter of the Queen of Ireland, to be the wife of *Marke*, King of Cornwall. A sailor, hidden in the rigging, sings a song to his Irish sweetheart which sets loose a tempest in the heart of the princess. In an outburst of rage she declares to her maid, *Brangäne*, that she will never set foot on Cornwall's shore; she deplores the impotency of her mother's sorcery over the wind and waves which she vainly invokes to dash the ship to pieces. *Brangäne* pleads to know the cause of her mistress's tumultuous disquiet and learns of the incidents which antedate those of which she is a present witness. Disguised as a harper and calling himself Tantris, *Tristan* had come to Ireland to be healed of a wound received in battle with Morold, Isolde's betrothed, whom he had killed and thus freed Cornwall from tribute to Ireland. *Isolde* nursed the stranger, but while doing so discovered one day that the edge of his sword was broken and that a splinter of steel taken from the head of her dead lover fitted into the nick in the sword's edge. Before her, at her mercy, lay the slayer of

him who was to have been her husband. She raised the sword to deal the avenging blow, but before it could descend the knight turned his glance upon her.
Not upon the threatening sword, but into her eyes did he look, and in a
flash her heart was empty of hate; an overwhelming love for him gushed
up within her. "After telling this tale to *Brangäne*, Isolde sends the maid
to summon *Tristan* to her presence; but the knight refuses to leave the helm
until he has brought the ship into harbor, and his squire, *Kurwenal*, incensed
at the tone addressed by the princess to one who, in his eyes, is the great-
est of heroes, as answer to the summons sings a stave of a popular ballad
which recounts the killing of Morold and the liberation of Cornwall by his
master. The refusal completes the desperation of *Isolde*. Outraged love, in-
jured personal and national pride (for she imagines that he who had relieved
Cornwall from tribute to Ireland was now gratifying his ambition by bringing her as Ireland's tribute to Cornwall), detestation of a loveless marriage
to 'Cornwall's weary king'—a thousand fierce but indefinable emotions are
seething in her heart. She resolves to die, and to drag *Tristan* down to death
with her. *Brangäne* unwittingly shows the way. She tries to quiet her mistress's fears of the dangers of a loveless marriage by telling her of a magic
potion brewed by the queen-mother, with which she will firmly attach
Marke to his bride. Thus innocently she takes the first step towards pre-
cipitating the catastrophe. *Isolde* demands to see the casket of magic phil-
tres, and finds that it also contains a deadly poison. *Kurwenal* enters to an-
nounce that the ship is in the harbor and *Tristan* desires her to prepare for
the landing. *Isolde* sends back greetings and a message that before she will
permit the knight to escort her before the king he must obtain from her
forgiveness for unforgiven guilt. Tristan obeys this second summons, and
in justification of his conduct in keeping himself aloof during the voyage
he, with great dignity, pleads his duty towards good morals, custom and
his king. *Isolde* reminds him of the wrong done her in the slaying of her
lover and her right to the vengeance which once she had renounced. *Tristan*
yields the right, and offers his sword and breast, but *Isolde* replies that she
cannot appear before *King Marke* as the slayer of his foremost knight, and
proposes that he drink a cup of reconciliation. *Tristan* sees one-half her purpose and chivalrously consents to pledge her in what he knows to be poison.
Isolde calls for the cup, which she had commanded *Brangäne* to prepare,
and when *Tristan* has drunk part of its contents she wrenches it from his
hand and drains it to the bottom. Thus they meet their doom, which is not
death and surcease of sorrow, but life and misery; for *Brangäne* had dis-
obeyed her mistress out of love, and mixed a love-potion instead of a death-
draught. A moment of bewilderment, and the two fated ones are in each
other's arms, pouring out an ecstasy of passion; then the maids of honor robe
Isolde to receive *King Marke*, who is coming on board to greet his bride."

Act II. Scene, a garden before *Queen Isolde's* chamber; time, a lovely night in summer. A torch burns in a ring beside the door leading from the chamber into the garden. The king has gone a-hunting, and the tones of his hunting-horns, answering each other, come floating on the night air. *Isolde* appears with *Brangäne* and pleads with her to extinguish the torch, thus giving a preconcerted signal to *Tristan*, who is waiting in concealment. "But *Brangäne* suspects treachery on the part of *Melot*, a knight who is jealous of *Tristan* and himself enamoured of *Isolde*, and who had planned the nocturnal hunt. She warns her mistress and begs her to wait. In their dialogue there is lovely fencing with the incident of the vanishing sounds of the hunt, like Shakespeare's dalliance with nightingale and lark in 'Romeo and Juliet.' To *Isolde* the horns are but the rustling of the forest leaves as they are caressed by the wind, or the purling and laughing of the brook. Longing has eaten up all patience, all discretion, all fear. She extinguishes the torch in spite of *Brangäne's* pleadings, and with wildly-waving scarf beckons on her hurrying lover. Beneath the foliage they sing their love through all the gamut of hope and despair." There is a rude interruption in the moment of their supremest ecstasy. *Kurwenal* dashes on the scene with sword drawn and a shout: "Save thyself, Tristan!" *King Marke*, his courtiers, and *Melot*, are at his heels. The aged king accuses his nephew and knight of treachery and bemoans his ingratitude and the loss of his love. From the words of the heart-torn king we learn that he had been forced into the marriage with *Isolde* by the disturbed state of his kingdom, and that he had not consented to it until *Tristan* (whose purpose it was to quiet the jealous anger of the Cornish barons) had threatened to depart from Cornwall unless the King revoked his decision to make him his successor. Tristan's answer to *Marke's* sorrowful upbraidings is to obtain a promise from *Isolde* that she will follow him into the "wondrous realm of night." Then he makes a feint of attacking *Melot*, but permits the traitor's sword to reach his side. He falls wounded unto death.

Act III. "The dignified, reserved knight of the first act, the impassioned lover of the second, is now a dream-haunted, longing, despairing, dying man, lying under a lime-tree in the yard of his ancestral castle in Brittany, wasting his last bit of strength in feverish fancies and ardent longings touching *Isolde*. *Kurwenal* has sent for her. Will she come? A shepherd tells of vain watches for the sight of a sail by playing a mournful melody on his pipe. Oh, the heart-hunger of the hero! The longing! Will she never come? The fever is consuming him, and his heated brain breeds fancies which one moment lift him above all memories of pain, and the next bring him to the verge of madness. Cooling breezes waft him again towards Ireland, whose princess healed the wound struck by Morold, then ripped it up again with the avenging sword with its telltale nick. From her hands he took the drink

(xii)

whose poison sears his heart. Accursed the cup and accursed the hand that brewed it! Will the shepherd never change his doleful strain? Ah, *Isolde*, how beautiful you are! The ship, the ship! It must be in sight. *Kurwenal*, have you no eyes? *Isolde's* ship! A merry tune bursts from the shepherd's pipe. It is the ship! What flag flies at the peak? The flag of 'All 's well!' Now the ship disappears behind a cliff. There the breakers are treacherous. Who is at the helm? Friend or foe? *Melot's* accomplice? Are you, too, a traitor, *Kurwenal*? *Tristan's* strength is unequal to the excitement of the moment. His mind becomes dazed. He hears *Isolde's* voice, and his wandering fancy transforms it into the torch whose extinction once summoned him to her side: '*Do I hear* the light?' He staggers to his feet and tears the bandages from his wound. 'Ha! my blood! flow merrily now! She who opened the wound is here to heal it!' Life endures but for one embrace, one glance, one word: 'Isolde!' While *Isolde* lies mortally stricken upon *Tristan's* corpse, *Marke* and his train arrive upon a second ship. *Brangäne* has told the secret of the love-draught, and the king has come to unite the lovers. But his purpose is not known, and faithful *Kurwenal* receives his death-blow while trying to hold the castle against *Marke's* men. He dies at *Tristan's* side. *Isolde*, unconscious of all these happenings, sings out her broken heart and expires.

> "'*And ere her ear might hear, her heart had heard,*
> *Nor sought she sign for witness of the word;*
> *But came and stood above him, newly dead,*
> *And felt his death upon her: and her head*
> *Bowed, as to reach the spring that slakes all drought;*
> *And their four lips became one silent mouth.*'"

H. E. KREHBIEL

Blue Hill, Maine, September 18, 1906.

ORDER OF THE SCENES

ACT I

ACT II

ACT III

TRISTAN AND ISOLDA

Tristan and Isolda.

Act I.

Introduction.

Richard Wagner.

Allmählich im Zeitmass etwas zurückhaltend.
Il tempo poco a poco ritenuto.

espress.

dim.

zart
dolce

cresc.

(The Curtain rises)

Scene I.

A marquee, richly hung with rugs, on the forward deck of a sailing-ship, at first entirely closed at the back; on one side a narrow companion-way leads to the cabin below.

Isolda on a couch, her head buried in the cushions. Brangæna, holding back a curtain, looks out over the side of the ship.

· travelling towards night

Mässig langsam.
Andante moderato.

The Voice of a young Sailor (from above, as if from the mast-head) *(kräftig) (energico)*

Tenor.

West-wärts schweift der Blick, ostwärts streicht das Schiff. Frisch
West-ward glanc-es sweep, east-ward steers the ship. The

weht der Wind der Hei-math zu:_ mein i-risch Kind, wo wei-lest du?
west-wind wild blows homeward now:_mine I-rish child,where ling'rest thou?

Sind's dei-ner Seuf-zer We-hen, die mir die Se-gel blä-hen?_
Or is it, thou art try-ing to fill the sails, by sigh-ing?_

We-he, we-he, du Wind!_ Weh, ach we-he, mein Kind!_
Blow then, wind fresh and wild!_ Woe, ah! woe is my child!_

I-ri-sche Maid,_____ du wil-de, min-ni-ge
Mine I-rish maid,_____ my wild and am-o-rous

Lebhaft.
Vivace.

Isolda (starting up quickly) (She looks round disturbed)

Maid! Wer wagt mich zu höh-nen?
maid! Who dares thus to mock me?

Mässig.
Moderato.

Brangä-ne, du?_ Sag', wo sind wir?
Brangæ-na, ho! Say, where are we?

schling's!
shreds!
Und was auf ihm
And what there-on

lebt, den we-henden A - them, den lass' ich euch Win - den zum
lives, their trem-u-lous life - breath, I leave to you winds for a

Brangæna (in great alarm and anxiety for Isolda)

Lohn! O weh! Ach! Ach des Ü-bels,das ich ge-
wage! Ah woe! Ah! Ah! This trouble long have I

ahnt!_ I - sol - de! Her - rin! Theu - res Herz! Was
feared!_ I - sol - da! La - dy! Dear - est heart! What

Allmählich etwas mässiger im Zeitmass.
Poco a poco più moderato.

bargst du mir so lang? Nicht ei - ne Thrä - ne wein-test du Va-ter und
keep'st thou hid so long? No tear at part - ing gav - est thou fa-ther or

Mut - ter; kaum ei - nen Gruss den Blei - ben - den bo - test
moth - er, and scarce a sign didst deign the for - sak - en

du: von der Hei - math schei - dend kalt und
ones: From thy home thou stol - est cold and

stumm, bleich und schwei - gend
dumb! Pale and si - lent

auf der Fahrt, oh - ne
all the way, ate'st thou

Nah - rung, oh - ne Schlaf,
no - - thing, sleep - less, too,

Scene II.

One now looks down the whole length of the ship to the helm, and over the stern across the sea to the horizon. In the centre, about the main-mast, are sailors, busied with ropes, and lying about; beyond them, in the stern, are knights and attendants similarly disposed; somewhat apart stands Tristan, his arms folded, gazing thoughtfully out over the sea; at his feet lounges Kurvenal. From the mast-head above, the voice of the young sailor is heard again.

Mässig langsam. Andante moderato.

The young Sailor (at the mast-head, invisible)

Frisch weht der Wind der Hei-math zu:_ mein
The west-wind wild blows home-ward now:_ mine

i-risch Kind, wo wei-lest du? Sind's dei-ner Seuf-zer We-hen,
I-rish child, where lin-g'rest thou? Or is it, thou art try-ing

die mir die Se-gel blä-hen? We-he, we-he, du Wind!
to fill the sails, by sigh-ing? Blow then, wind fresh and wild!

Isolda (whose eyes have at once sought Tristan and fixed stonily on him_ aside, gloomily)

Mir er-ko-ren,_ mir ver-lo-ren,_
I mis-tak-en! I for-sak-en!_

Weh, ach we-he, mein Kind!
Woe, ah woe is my child!

16

wann!
bride!_

Dünkt es dich dun-kel, mein Gedicht? Frag'ihn denn
Think'st thou,there's naught in what I say? He is a

selbst,den frei-en Mann, ob mir zu nah'n er wagt? Der Eh - ren Gruss und zücht'-ge
man, go ask him,then, if come to me he dare? This cai - tiff lord doth e'en neg-

(etwas gedehnt)
(poco steso)

Acht vergisst der Her - rin der za-ge Held, dass ihr Blick ihn nur nicht er -
lect to greet his la _ dy with due re - spect; For he wants not her eye to

rei - che, den Hel - den oh - ne Glei - che!_ O,___ er weiss wohl, wär -
catch him, this knight with none to match him! Oh,___ he knows why it

um!_
is!_

Zu dem Stol-zen geh', meld'ihm der Her-rin Wort! Meinem Dienst be -
Now to this Sir Pride bear you his la - dy's will! As my vas - sal

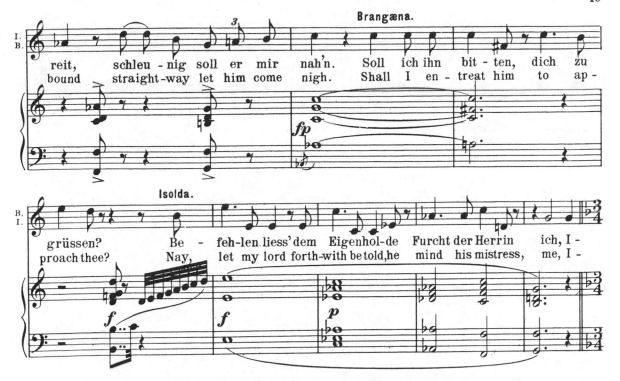

Brangæna.

reit, schleu - nig soll er mir nah'n. Soll ich ihn bit - ten, dich zu
bound straight-way let him come nigh. Shall I en - treat him to ap-

Isolda.

grüssen? Be - feh-len.liess'dem Eigenhol-de Furcht der Herrin ich, I -
proach thee? Nay, let my lord forth-with be told,he mind his mistress, me, I -

(At a gesture of command from Isolda, Brangæna leaves her, and hesitatingly
makes her way along the deck, past the busy sailors, to the stern; Isolda gazes
after her with a blank expression, and throws herself back on the couch, and so
remains, during what follows, her eyes steady fixed astern)

Gemächlich.
Comodo.

sol - de!
sol - da!

(Kurvenal sees Brangæna coming and, without rising, twitch-
es Tristan's cloak)

Flu - ren dem Blick noch blau sich fär - ben, harrt mein Kò - nig
mead - ows from dis - tance still are a - zure, for my la - dy

mei - ner Frau: zu ihm sie zu ge - lei - ten, bald nah' ich mich der Lichten;
waits my King: and soon to lead her to him, will I at - tend her Highness;

Brangæna.

Mein Her - re Tristan, hö - re wohl: dei - ne
My lord, Sir Tristan, hear, I pray: in her

Keinem gönnt' ich die - se Gunst.
I this guer - don grant to none.

Dienste will die Frau, dass du zur Stell' ihr nah - test, dort, wo sie dei - ner harrt.
service, she demands that you forthwith approach her, there where she waits for thee.

Auf je - der
In ev - 'ry

So, hiess sie, sollt' ich sa - gen:— Be -
Thus, said she, should I tell thee, "Nay,

Gedehnt.
Steso.

feh - len liess' dem Ei - genhol - de Furcht der Her-rin sie, I -
let my lord forth-with be told, he mind his mistress, me, I -

Lebhaft, doch nicht zu schnell.
Vivace, ma non troppo presto.   **Tristan** (quietly)

sol - de.   Was wohl er - wi - der-test du?
sol - da!"   What an-swer think'st thou to make?

Kurvenal (springing up)

Darf ich die Antwort sa - gen?
May I sup-ply the an-swer?

Kurvenal.

Das sa - ge sie der Frau I - sold':   Wer Kornwalls Kron' und
This shall she say to Dame I - sold':   If England's fee and

Eng - lands Erb' an Ir - lands Maid vermacht, der kann der Magd nicht
Corn - wall's crown to Ireland's maid are due, she can - not be the

ei - gen sein, die selbst dem Ohm er schenkt. Ein Herr der Welt,
giv - er's own, and be his un - cle's, too. A Man of Fate,

Tri - stan der Held! Ich ruf's: du sag's, und groll - ten mir tau - send Frau I - sol -
Tris - tan the Great! I've said: an there should scold us a thousand Dame I - sol -

(While Tristan by gestures tries to silence him, and Brangæna, offended, turns to
go away, Kurvenal, as she moves slowly away, sings after her at the top of his
voice)

Schneller.
Più mosso.

den. „Herr Morold zog zu Mee - re her, in
das. "To lay a tax on Cornish backs Sir

K. Kornwall Zins zu ha - ben; ein Eiland schwimmt auf ö - dem Meer, da liegt er nun be-
Mo - rold once was fer - ried; 'mid tussocks damp, in dis-mal swamp, his bod - y now lies

K. gra - - ben! Sein Haupt doch hängt im I - ren - land, als
bur - - ied! His head, tho', went to I - rish lands, as

K. Zins gezahlt von En - ge - land. Hei! unser Held Tri-stan, wie der Zins zah - len
tax - es sent by English hands. Here's to my lord Tris-tan! For a tax, he's the

(Kurvenal, driven away by Tristan, goes below to the cabin; Brangæna, much disturbed,
comes back to Isolda, and closes the curtains behind her while the whole crew is heard
singing without)

K. kann!"
man!"

Tenor.

Noch etwas beschleunigend
Ancora più mosso

All the Men. "Sein Haupt doch hängt im I - ren - land, als Zins gezahlt von
Bass. His head, tho', went to I - rish lands, as tax - es sent by

Scene III.

(Isolda and Brangæna alone; the curtains are again completely closed)
(Isolda rises with a despairing gesture of wrath. Brangæna falls at her feet)

Isolda (restraining herself from a furious outbreak)

Brangæna.

Doch nun von Tristan! Ge-nau will ich's ver-nehmen. Ach, fra-ge nicht!
What now of Tristan? Tell all! for I must hear it! Oh, ask me not!

ff — dim. — p trem.

Isolda. — Brangæna.

Frei sag's oh-ne Furcht! Mit höf'-schen Wor-ten wich er
Come, speak without fear! With court-ly phrase he par-ried

p — p — p — p

Doch als du deut-lich mahntest?
But when you told him clear-ly?

aus. Da ich zur Stell' ihn zu dir rief:
all. When I had bid him come forth-with:

cresc. — mf

wo er auch steh', so sagte er, getreu-lich dien' er ihr, der Frauen höchster
What-e'er he did, said he to me, he tru-ly served thee well, the crown of wo-man-

sf — sf dim. — p — dolce

sin - gen, wohl könnt' auch ich er - wi - dern!
gainst me! Ah! but I too could an - swer!

Mässiger.
Più moderato.

Von ei - nem Kahn, der klein und arm an
A - bout the skiff, so small, so poor, that

poco rall.
dim.
p

Irlands Kü - sten schwamm, da - rinnen krank ein sie - cher Mann e - lend
came to Ire - land's shore! And in it lay a wounded man, help - less

im Ster - ben lag. I - sol - de's Kunst ward ihm be -
and dy - ing there. I - sol - da's skill he learned to

kannt, mit Heil - sal - ben und Bal - sam - saft der
know; with salves sooth - ing, and heal - ing balms, the

Wun - de, die ihn plag - te, ge-treu-lich pflag sie da. Der
wounds that so dis-tressed___ him she tend-ed faith-ful-ly. As

Immer belebter.
Sempre più animato.

„Tan - tris" mit sor-gen-der List sich nann-te, als
"Tan - tris" he cun-ning-ly had dis-guised him! As

Schneller.
Più mosso.

„Tri - stan" I - sold' ihn bald er-kann - te, da in des
"Tris - tan" I - sold' soon rec-og-nized him: His sword when

Müss' - gen Schwer - te ei - ne Scharte sie ge-wahr - te, da-rin ge-
turn - ing o - ver, there a nick she did dis-cov - er, where fit-ted

nau sich fügt' ein Split - ter, den einst im Haupt des I - ren-
fair and square a sliv - er that in the head of Ire - land's

Nun hör', wie ein Held —— Ei - de
Now hear, how a knight —— keeps his

hält!
oath!

Den als Tan - tris un - er-kannt ich ent-
For as Tan - tris, un - re-vealed, I re-

las - sen, als Tri - stan kehrt er kühn zu - rück;
leased him, as Tris - tan comes he brave-ly back;

auf stol - zem Schiff, von ho - hem Bord, Ir - lands
and from his ship, so proud and high, Ire - land's

Etwas gedehnt.
Poco steso.

Er bin begehrt' er zur Eh' für Kornwalls mü-den Kö-nig, für
heir - ess he asks as a bride, for Corn-wall's ser-vile rul-er, his

rallent. Schnell.
Vivo.

Mar-ke, sei-nen Ohm. Da Mo - rold
an-cient un-cle Mark. Were Mo - rold

leb - te, wer hätt' es ge - wagt, uns
liv - ing, who ev - er had dared to

je sol - che Schmach zu bie - ten? Für der zins - - pflicht' - gen
put such a slight up - on us, as that pay - - er of

Kor - nen-Für - sten um Ir - lands Kro - ne zu wer - ben!
Corn - ish trib - ute for Ire - land's crown should be suit - or!

Schnell.
Allegro.

mit ihr gab er es preis!
to her he dared re-veal!

Wie sieg - prangend, heil und hehr,
How mas - ter-ful, brave and bold,

laut und hell wies er auf mich:
turned he all eyes up on me!

Etwas mässiger.
Poco più moderato.

„Das wär'
"A trea -

- ein Schatz, mein Herr und Ohm; wie
- sure she, my liege and coz; what

(She draws Isolda

toward the couch)

Immer noch sehr bewegt.
Sempre con molto moto.

46

(She comes toward Isolda coaxingly and caressingly)

Wo
Where

leb - -te der Mann, der dich nicht lieb - te? der I - sol -
lives there a man that would not love thee? He that sees___

- -den säh', und in I- -sol- -den se-
___ I - sol- - -da, would he not too glad- -

lig nicht ganz_____ ver - ging'? Doch.
ly in love_____ ex - pire? And

der dir er - ko - ren, wär' er so kalt,
he that thou choos-est, waxed he e'er cold,

Etwas langsamer.
Poco più lento.

Isolda (darkly)

Der Mut - ter Rath gemahnt mich
My mother's arts I know full

recht;   willkom - men preis' ich ih - re Kunst:___
well,   and glad - ly now I welcome them:___

Ra - che   für den Ver - rath,___   Ruh' in der   Noth___ dem
Ven-geance   for trea-son   they,___   rest___ when the   heart___ is

Brangæna.

Herzen!___   Den Schreindort bring'mir her!   Er   birgt,___ was heil___ dir
troubled!   That cas - ket fetch me here!   Here   lies___ a   cure___ for

Scene IV.

(Through the curtains enters Kurvenal unceremoniously)

Tri - stan brin - ge mei - nen Gruss, und meld' ihm, was ich
Tris - tan may'st thou greet from me, and say how I have

sa - ge. Sollt' ich zur Seit' ihm ge - hen, vor Kö - nig Mar - ke zu
spo - ken: If I should walk be - side him, when to his monarch he

ste -hen, nicht möcht' es nach Zucht und Fug ge - scheh'n, em -
hied him, then would it be nei - ther meet nor right, un -

pfing' ich Süh - ne nicht zu - vor für un - -ge-sühnte Schuld:
less I first had par - doned him for what of-fense he gave:

(Kurvenal makes a gesture of defiance)

drum such' er mei - ne Huld.
So let him par - don crave.

60

Brangæna (throwing herself at Isolda's feet)

Süh — — ne!
pledge — — me!

Entset — — zen!
O hor — — ror!

Isolda (with great vehemence)

Scho — ne mich Ar - me!
Pit — y, I pray thee!

Scho — — ne du
Pit — — y thou

mich, un - treu - e Magd!_
me, O faith-less maid!_

Allmählich etwas zurückhaltend.
Poco a poco ritenuto.

Kennst du der Mut-ter Kün-ste nicht?
Know'st thou not well my mother's skill?

Wähnst du, die Al - les klug er -
Think'st thou that she, who all_ fore-

wägt, oh - ne Rath in fremdes Land hätt' sie mit dir mich ent-
sees, un - pre-pared had bid-den me to seek far coun-tries with

(Kurvenal retires again. Brangæna, scarcely mistress of herself, turns towards the back. Isolda, summoning all her powers to meet the crisis, walks slowly and with effort to the couch, leaning on the head of which she then stands, her eyes fixed on the entrance.)

(Tristan enters and pauses respectfully at the entrance)

(Isolda, a prey to violent agitation, gazes on him intently)

Tristan.

Begehrt, Her-rin, was ihr wünscht.
Command, la-dy, what you wish.

Isolda.

Wüss-test du nicht, was ich be-geh-re, da doch die
Tho' un-a-ware what were my wishes, was it not

Furcht, mir's zu er-fül-len, fern mei-nem Blick dich hielt?
fear to un-der-take them, kept thee from out my sight?

Tristan.   Isolda.

Ehrfurcht hielt mich in Acht. Der Eh-re
Hon-our held me in awe. Small hon-our,

we-nig bo-test du mir; mit off'-nem Hohn ver-wehrtest du Ge-
tru-ly, gav-est thou me; with sheer con-tempt hast thou re-fused o-

Blut-schuld schwebt zwi-schen uns. Die ward gesühnt. Nicht zwischen
'Twixt us blood - guilt-i - ness! That was for-giv'n. Not be-tween

Tristan. Isolda.

uns!
us!

Tristan.

Im off'-nen Feld, vor al-lem Volk ward
In o-pen field, 'fore all the folk, a

Etwas bewegter, doch mässig.
Poco più mosso, ma moderato.

Isolda.

Ur - feh - de ge - schwo-ren. Nicht da war's, wo ich
feud - truce has been sworn to. 'Twas not then that I

Tan - tris barg, wo Tri - stan mir ver-fiel. Da
Tan - tris hid and Tris - tan hos-tage held. Then

stand er herr - lich, hehr und heil;
stood he lord - ly, brave and bright;

dolce

doch was er schwur, das schwur ich nicht:— zu
yet what he swore, that swore not I:— I

schwei-gen hatt' ich ge-lernt. Da in stil-ler
school'd my-self to be still. In my qui-et

Belebend.
Animando.

Kam-mer krank er lag,
cham-ber sick he lay,

mit dem Schwer-te stumm ich vor ihm stund:
with his sword I stood be-fore him, dumb:

schwieg da mein Mund,
No word I spoke,

sorgt' ich schlecht um dei - nen Her - ren; was wür - de Kö - nig Mar - ke
ill a turn I'd do thy mas-ter! How, think you now, King Mark would

sa - gen, er-schlüg' ich ihm den be - sten Knecht, der Kron' und Land ihm ge -
take it, if I should slay his fore-most man, who won him king - dom and

menial servant (perj.)

wann, den al - ler-treu'-sten Mann?
rights, the best of all his knights?

Dünkt dich so
Think'st thou so

we - nig, was er dir dankt, bringst du die I - rin ihm— als Braut, dass er nicht
small his thanks be to thee, thou that hast brought me as— his bride, he'd not be

schöl - te, schlüg' ich den Wer - ber, der Ur - feh-de-Pfand so treu ihm lie-fert zur
an - ger'd, slew I the woo - er, who brings him so good a pledge of truce to the

ha! he! ha!
O! heave O!

Tenor II. *ff*
Am O - ber - mast die Se - gel ein!
Stand by the top! Haul down the sail!

Ho! he! ha! he!
Yo! heave O! hey!

Bass II. *ff*
Ho! he! ha! he! ho! he! ha! he!
Yo! heave O! heave O! heave O! hey!

Tristan (starting from his moody silence) **Isolda.**

Wo sind wir? Hart am
Where are we? Right at

Ziel! Tri - stan, ge - winn' ich Süh - ne? Was
land! Tris - tan, is peace be - tween us? What

hast du mir zu sa - gen?
an - swer dost thou make me?

Bass I. II.

Ho! he! ha! he!
Yo! heave O! hey!

(On an impatient sign from Isolda, Bran-

gæna hands her the full goblet)

Isolda (advancing with the cup to Tristan, who gazes fixedly

Du hörst den Ruf?
Thou hear'st the call?

in her eyes)

Wir sind am Ziel:
We are at land:

in kur- zer
be- fore King

rallent.

(very earnestly)

(with veiled scorn)

Frist steh'n wir vor Kö- nig
Mark we shall ere- long be

Etwas gedehnt.
Poco steso.

Mar- ke.
standing.

Ge- lei- test du mich, dünkt dich's nicht
And lead'st thou me then, were it not

lieb, darfst du so ihm sa - gen:
well, if thou thus couldst greet him:

„Mein Herr und Ohm, sieh' die dir
"My lord and king, look well on

an: ein sanf-t'res Weib gewannst du nie. Ih - ren
her: a ten - d'rer wife thou ne'er couldst win. Her be-

An - ge-lob - ten er - schlug ich ihr einst, sein Haupt sandt' ich ihr
troth - ed lov - er I slew, of a truth; his head I sent her

So gu-ter Ga-ben hol-der Dank schuf mir ein sü-sser Süh-ne-
Such good-ly gifts I have to thank, with her a draught of truce I

trank; den bot mir ih - re Huld zu
drank; that par-don for me won, for

Sehr bewegt.
Molto animato.

süh - nen al - le Schuld."
all the wrong I'd done."

Sailors (without)
Tenor.

Auf das Tau!
Ca - ble out!

Bass.

cresc.

To T's honor, highest toast! To his anguish highest defiance!

89

Trembling seizes them. They clutch their hearts tightly _____

Etwas bewegt.
Poco mosso.

_____ and then pass their hands over
their brows. _____
rall.

Langsam.
Lento.

Again try to meet each other's
eyes _____

sehr ausdrucksvoll
molto espress.

_____ lower their eyes in confusion, then raise then again to each

other with increasing longing.)

92

(Brangæna, who with averted face was leaning bewildered and trembling over the side of the ship, now turns and sees the lovers clasped in each other's arms, and rushes forward, wringing her hands in despair)

Tristan.

O Won - ne vol - ler Tü - cke! O trug-ge- weih - - tes
O joy with false-ness freighted! O bliss fraud-con - - se -

(People have climbed aboard; others have rigged a gangway; their behavior indicates
their expectation of the coming arrival)

Glücke!
crat-ed!

All the Men.   Tenor.

(General outburst Korn - wall   Heil!
of rejoicing)   Corn - wall   hail!

Bass.

(Trumpets on the Stage)

(The Curtain falls quickly)

(The Curtain rises.)

upside down torch, held by Eros, is death

Scene I.

(A garden with high trees before the chamber of Isolda, which lies at one side and is approached by steps. Bright and inviting summer night. A torch burns by the open door. A hunter's horn is heard. Brangæna, standing on the steps, is watching the retreating hunt, which can still be heard)

(Horns on the Stage.)

(Brangæna looks anxiously into the chamber where she sees Isolda coming)

112

hold; des Quel-les sanft rie - seln-de Wel - le rauscht so
sweet. The wa-ter I hear__ in the well there, flow - ing

won - - nig da - her. Wie hört' ich sie, tos'- ten noch
soft - - ly a - way. If horns still blew, how could I

Hör-ner? Im Schwei - - - gen der
hear it? In si - - - lence at

Nacht nur_ lacht mir__ der Quell:__
night a - lone sings__ the well.__

der mei - ner harrt_____ in
My lov'd one waits_____ in

zart
dolce
p
pp

zart
p dolce
pp

blö-det für euch?
watching on you!

Da dort an Schiffes Bord, von Tristan's
That day when there on board, from Tristan's

be-ben-der Hand, die blei-che Braut, kaum ih-rer mächtig, Kö-nig Mar-ke em-
trem-u-lous hands King Mark received his fair-ly fainting, pale and pas-sion-less

pfing,
bride:

als Al-les ver-wirrt auf die Wan-ken-de sah, der güt'-ge
when all were a-ghast and were gaz-ing on thee, the gracious

Kö-nig, mild be-sorgt, die Mü-hen der lan-gen Fahrt, die du
mon-arch's kind con-cern to wear-i-ness of the way thou hadst

lit-test, laut be-klagt:— ein Einz'ger war's, ich ach-tet' es wohl,—
journeyed, laid the blame. But one there was— I not-ed it well,—

trügst! Ist es nicht Tri-stan's treu - e-ster Freund? Muss mein
ceived! Is he not Tris-tan's faith-ful-lest friend? When my

Trau - ter mich mei - den, dann weilt er bei
lov - er must leave me, he lin - gers with

dolce

Brangæna.

Me - lot al - lein. Was mir ihn ver-dächtig, macht dir ihn
Me - lot a - lone. For what I distrust him, to thee he's

theu - er! Von Tristan zu Mar-ke ist Me-lot's Weg; dort
dear - er! From Tristan to Mark 'tis, that Me-lot goes; there

sä't er üb - le Saat. Die heut' im Rath dies nächtli-che
sows he e - vil seed. And those who now this e-ven-ing

Ja-gen so ei - lig schnell be-schlossen, einem edlern Wild, als dein Wähnen
hunting arranged with so much hur-ry, 'tis a high-er game, than you wit, they

meint, gilt ih-re Jä - gers - list.
deem worthy their hunts-man - ship.

Isolda.

Dem Freund zu
For friend-ship's

Lieb'__ er-fand die - se List __ aus Mit - leid
sake __ the plan was de - vised; __ so helps Sir

Me - lot, der Freund. Nun willst du den Treu - en
Me - lot his friend. Now wouldst thou this friend - ship

schel - ten? Bes - ser als du __ sorgt er für mich;
slan - der? Bet - ter than thou __ cares he for me!

nahm ich's vermessen zur Hand,
I rash-ly took to my hand;

Frau
Love's

Min - - ne hat es mei - ner Macht ent-
god - - dess un - to me did coun - ter-

wandt. Die Tod - ge-weih-te nahm sie in Pfand, fass-te das Werk in ih - re
mand. Death's vic-tims then she took as her own; now by her hand the work be

Sehr zurückhaltend.
Molto ritardando.

Mässig bewegt.
Moderato con moto.

Hand. Wie sie es wen - - det,
done! Wher - e'er she guides it,

wie sie es en - - det, was sie mir küh - - re,
how she de-cides it, what rood she reads me,

hör' mein Fle - hen! Der Ge-fahr leuch - ten-des Licht,
do my bid - ding! Danger yet looks from the light:

nur heu - te, heut! die
this once, this once! Quench

Immer bewegter.
Sempre più mosso.

Isolda.

Fa-ckel dort lö-sche nicht! Die im Bu - sen
not the torch for to-night! She that kin - dles

mir die Gluth ent - facht,
thus my soul's de - sire,

die mir das Her - ze bren - nen
she that my heart has set on

128

(She takes the torch from the doorway)

Licht verscheuchte. Zur War-te du: dort wa-che treu! Die
light doth banish. Go thou on guard, and watch thou well! The

Leuch - - - te, und wär's meines Le-bens Licht,
torch here, and were it my light of life,

lach - - end sie zu lö-schen zag' ich
smil - - ing I should quench it, with - out

(She throws the torch to the ground, where it gradually goes out)

nicht!
strife.

(Brangæna turns distressedly away in order to get upon the roof by an outer staircase,

where she slowly disappears)

(Isolda listens and looks, at first timidly, down the avenue of trees)

(Stirred by increasing longing, she goes nearer to the avenue and looks out more boldly)

(She waves her kerchief, at first from time to

time, then oftener, finally with passionate impatience, faster and faster.)

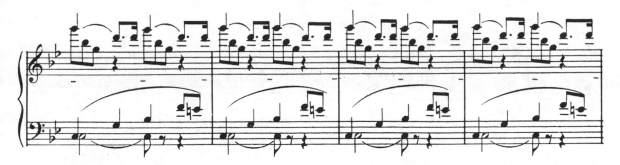

Immer bewegter.
Sempre più animato.

(A gesture of sudden delight shows that she has perceived her lover in the

distance. She raises herself higher and higher, the better to overlook the place, then hurries back

to the steps, from the top of which she beckons to him as he approaches)

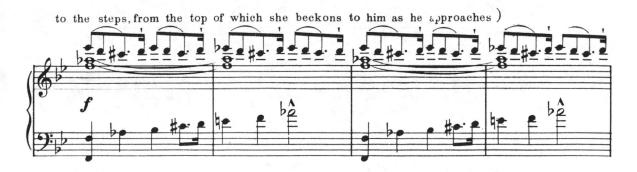

Scene II.
Tristan and Isolda.

Tristan (rushing in)

I - sol - - - de!
I - sol - - - da!

Isolda.

Tri - - stan! Ge - lieb - - ter!
Tris - - tan! Be - lov - - ed!

Ge - lieb - - te!
Be - lov - - ed!

(Embracing wildly,

they come down the stage)

sempre
immer f

ffff

dem tü — — cki — schen Ta — — ge, dem
With treach — — er — y freight — — ed, our

här — — te — sten Fein — — de Hass und
bit — — ter — est foe, so feared and

Immer sehr schnell.
Sempre molto presto.

Kla — — ge! Wie du das
hat — — ed! As with this

Licht, ___ o könnt' ich die Leuch — — te, der
link, ___ I'd deal with all day — — — light, our

Lie — be Lei — den zu rä — chen, dem
lov — ing long — ings a — veng — ing, the

frechen Ta — ge ver —
gar — ish day — light by

Glanz und Licht, I - sol - den mir ent - rückt'! Was mir das
ray and light it barr'd I - sold' from me! What my en-

Au - ge so ent - zückt', _____ mein Her - ze tief zur
tranc - ed eyes might see, _____ my heart must crush to

Er - - de drückt': in lich - ten Ta - ges Schein wie
earth for thee: For while that light should shine, how

Isolda.

war I - sol - de mein? War sie nicht
might I - sold' be mine? Was she not

(Der Bass möglichst gehalten.)
(Il basso molto tenuto.)

dein, die dich er - kor? _____ Was
thine, when thee I chose? _____ What

al - lem Heer;   vor_ al - lem Vol - ke___ pries ich laut der
I de _ clare,   to_ all man-kind thy___ praise I cried as

cresc.   f   p   cresc.

Er ___ de schön ___ ste ___ Kö ___ nigs-
Earth's ___ most fair and ___ queen - ly

f   -   -   -pìu f   ff

Immer sehr lebhaft.
Sempre molto vivace.

Braut.   Dem Neid,___ den mir der Tag   er-
bride.   The hate___ this day-light did   a-

kräftig gestossen
staccato con forza

ff   più f

weckt';   dem Ei - fer,   den mein Glü - cke schreckt';   der
wake,   the en-vy   that my peace   could shake,   the

f   p   cresc. _   _   _   _   _

Missgunst, die mir Eh - ren   und Ruhm be-gann zu   schwe-ren:
cov-et - ous fore - bod - ing   that hon-our was cor - rod - ing:___

f   p   cresc. _   _   _   -sf cresc. _   _   _

152

T. sei-nen prah - len-den Schein ver - lacht, wem die Nacht den
and its glit - ter-ing light, are flout - ed by all that

T. Blick ge - weiht: sei-nes fla-ckernden Lich - tes flüchti - ge
love the night. For its flick-er - ing beams, so fit-ful - ly

T. Blit-ze blen - - den uns nicht mehr. Wer des To- -des
flashing, blind our eyes no more. Who the night of

T. Nacht lie-bend er-schaut, wem sie ihr tief Ge-heim-niss ver-
death lov-ing-ly scan, those who have gazed on her se- -cret

T. traut: des Ta - ges Lü - gen, Ruhm und Ehr, Macht und Ge-
plan, will hold false day-light's rank and name, hon - our and

162

Langsamer, und allmählich immer langsamer.
Rallentando sempre poco a poco.

Lie - bes - won - ne ihm lacht.
love and pas - sion in - vite!

(Tristan draws Isolda gently down

on a flowery bank at one side, sinks on his knees before her and rests his head on her arm)

Mässig langsam.
Lento moderato.

nimm mich auf___ in dei-nen Schoss,
lift,__ oh, lift__ us up to thee!

lö - se von der Welt mich
from the world now set us

Schoss,
thee!

lö - se von der Welt mich los!
from the world now set us free!

Tristan.

los!   Ver - lo - schen nun die letz - - te Leuch - te;
free!   For van - ished are the light's___ last gleam - -ings,

Isolda.

was   wir   dach - -ten,   was   uns däuch - te;
All   that   daunt- -ed,   all   that haunt- -ed,

Isolda.

all'   Ge - mah - -nen,
all   our grop- -ing,

Tristan.

all'   Ge - den - -ken,
all   our seem- -ing,

(Completely carried away, Tristan and Isolda sink down and remain lying on the flowery bank, their heads side by side)

171

Die sechs ♪ genau den sechs ♪ des frühern $\frac{3}{4}$ *Takts entsprechend.*
The six ♪ exactly equivalent to those of the $\frac{3}{4}$ *movement before.*

stür-ben wir, um un - ge-trennt, e -wig ei -nig,
might we die as ne'er to part, aye u - nit - ed,

oh - ne End', ohn' Er - wa - chen, ohn' Er - ban-gen,
ne'er ___ to end, ne'er to wak - en, peace un-bound-ed,

(gesteigert)
(accrescendo)

na - men - los in Lieb' ___ um-fan-gen, ganz uns selbst ge-
name - less there by love ___ sur-round - ed, each to oth - er

Isolda (looking up at him in thoughtful absorption)

So stür-ben wir, um un - ge-
So might we die as ne'er ___ to

ge - ben, der Lie-be nur zu le - ben!
giv - ing, for love a - lone there liv - ing!

186

188

Scene III.

Sehr schnell (♩ merklich schneller als zuvor).
Prestissimo (♩ perceptibly quicker than before).

(Mark, Melot and courtiers, in hunting-dress, come quickly from the avenue towards the front, and pause

Wieder das vorhergehende Hauptzeitmass (♩ mässiger).
The previous tempo (♩ slower).
Sehr lebhaft. Molto vivace.

in amazement before the lovers. In the meantime Brangæna descends from the turret, and rushes towards

Isolda, who, with instinctive shame, leans with averted face upon the flowery bank. Tristan, with an e-

qually instinctive movement, with one arm spreads his cloak so as to conceal Isolda from the eyes of the

newcomers.— In this position he remains for some time, his eyes steadily fixed upon the men who look at

him with varied emotions.— Morning dawns)

Allmählich etwas langsamer.
Poco a poco allargando.

Mässig bewegt.
Con moto moderato.

Tristan. Melot (to Mark)

Der ö - de Tag_ zum letz - ten Mal! Das_
The day has dawned_ and 'tis the last! Now,

_ sollst du, Herr, mir sa - gen, ob_ ich ihn recht ver-klagt? Das dir zum
_ good my lord, I ask you, have_ I ac-cused him right? I said I'd

Pfand ich gab, ob ich mein Haupt ge-wahrt? Ich zeigt' ihn dir in off'-ner
stake my head,_ well, have I saved it now? Thou'st seen him in the fla-grant

sf p poco cresc.

That. Namen und Ehr' hab' ich ge-treu vor Schan-de dir be-
act! Honour and fame, thanks to my faith, I've shield-ed thee from

f

Mässig langsam.
Lento moderato.

Mark (violently affected, then with trembling voice)

wahrt. Tha-test du's wirklich? Wähnst du das?_
shame. Hast thou tho', tru - ly? Think'st thou so?

sehr ausdrucksvoll

molto espressivo

dim.

f p p

sehr getragen
con molto portamento

Sieh' ihn dort, den
See him there, the

Treu'sten al-ler Treu-en;   blick' auf ihn,_ den freundlichsten der
tru - est of the trust-ed.   look on him,_ whose friend-ship was the

Freunde: sei-ner Treu- e frei'-ste That traf mein
firm-est!   Yet his friendliest deed to me smote my

Herz mit feindlichstem Ver - rath!_____
heart with deadliest treacher - y!_____

Trog mich Tristan,   sollt' ich hof-fen, was sein Trü - gen mir ge-
Trick'd by Tristan!   Shall I flat-ter what his treach - er-y could

- stan sie ver - lor? Die Tri - stan sich zum Schild er-kor, wo-hin ist
- tan's lost them all? The vir - tue Tris-tan took for shield, where is that

riten.
f *riten.* *p* *ten.* *cresc.*

Breit. Largamente.

rallent. (langsam) (lento)

Tu-gend nun ent-floh'n, da mei-nen Freund sie flieht, da Tri - stan mich ver-
vir-tue van - ish'd now, that from him fell a - way, and Tris - tan can be-

f *rallent.* *dim.* *p* *p*

Wieder mässig langsam.
Lento moderato, come prima.

(Tristan slowly drops his eyes to the ground; his face expresses his increasing sorrow as Mark continues.)

rieth?
tray?

p *ausdrucksvoll und weich*
espressivo e dolce *p* *f*

Belebend.
Animando.

Wo - zu die Dienste oh - ne Zahl, der Eh - ren
What was thy ser-vice all un-told, that hon - our,

p *p*

Ruhm, der Grö-sse Macht, die Mar - - ken du ge-wannst; musst' Ehr' und
fame and pow'r of place thou won'st — for Mark, the King? Must hon - our,

poco cresc. *p* *cresc.* -

Mehr belebend.
Più animando.

Ruhm, Gröss' und Macht, muss-te die Dien-ste oh-ne Zahl dir Mar -
fame, power and place, must all thy ser-vic-es un-told, by Mark's ____

- ke's Schmach be - zah-len?   Dünk - te zu
- dis-grace be paid for?   Thought ye so

we - nig dich sein Dank, dass, was du ihm er - wor-ben, Ruhm und
lit - tle worth his thanks, that all that you had won him, fame and

Reich, er zu Erb' und Ei - - gen dir gab?
for - tune, he made you heir to it all?

Da kin - der-los einst schwand sein Weib, so liebt' er
When child-less his wife he had lost, so loved he

dich, dass nie auf's Neu' sich Mar - ke wollt' ver - mäh-len.
thee, that ne'er a - new could Mark e'er wish to mar-ry.

mf *dim.* *p*

Belebt. Con moto.

Da al-lesVolk zu Hof und Land mit Bitt'_ und Dräu - en in ihn drang, die
When all the country, all the court with pray'rs and threats a-round him throng'd, a

p *cresc. -*

Kö - ni-gin dem Lan-de, die Gat-tin sich zu kie - sen; da sel - ber
queen to give the country, him-self a wife to take him, when thou thy-

f *dim.* *p*

du den Ohm beschworst, des Ho - fes Wunsch, des Lan - des Wil - len güt -
self didst ev - er urge that what the court and coun - try want-ed, gra -

p *cresc. -*

- lich zu er-fül-len: in Wehr wi - der Hof und Land, inWehr selbst ge-gen
- cious-ly be granted: ar - rayed 'gainst the court and folk, array'd a - gainst thy-

mf *p* *cresc. -* *f*

- - mel er - löst, war - um mir die - se Höl - le?
- - I may win, why this hell do I suf - fer?

riten. *a tempo*

Die kein E - - - lend sühnt, war - um
If no ills it soothe, why

rall. *molto rall.*

um mir die - se Schmach? Den
falls the pain on me? Whence

Sehr langsam.
Molto adagio.

a tempo

sehr ausdrucksvoll
molto espressivo

(*weich*)
(*dolce*)

un - er - forsch - lich tief ge - heimniss - vol - len Grund, wer macht der Welt ihn
un - dis - cov - er'd, deep, mys - te - rious causes flow, who e'er the world shall

langsam.
adagio.

Langsam.
Adagio.

Tristan (raising his eyes sympathizingly to Mark)

kund? O Kö - nig, das kann ich dir nicht
show? O monarch! That can I nev - er

meint, der Son-ne Licht nicht scheint: es ist das dun - kel - mächt' - ge
mind, the sun-light doth not find; it is the dark - some land of

Land, da - raus die Mut - ter mich ent-sandt, als, den im To - de sie em-
night, where me my moth - er brought to light, and as in death she did con-

pfan - gen, im Tod sie liess an das Licht_____ ge - lan - gen.
ceive me, in death to lan-guish in light_____ did leave me.

Was, da sie mich ge - bar, ihr Lie - bes - ber - ge
What did shield her from earth, what time she gave me

war, das Wun-der-reich der Nacht, aus der ich einst er-
birth, the deep and won-drous night, that once I left for

211

Lebhaftes Zeitmass.
Tempo vivo.

Melot (drawing his sword)

Ver-räther! Ha! Zur Ra - che, Kö-nig! Dul-dest du die-se Schmach?
Thou traitor! Ha! A-venge thee, monarch! Canst thou bear this affront?

Tristan (draws his sword and turns quickly round)

Wer wagt sein Le - ben an das mei - ne?
Who's he will risk his life a - gainst me?

(Fixing his gaze on Melot)

Mein Freund war
My friend was

der, er minn-te mich hoch und theu-er;　um
he, and tru-ly and well he loved me;　my

Ehr' und Ruhm mir war er be-sorgt wie
name and fame were dear-er to him than

214

Wieder lebhaft.
Vivace, come prima.

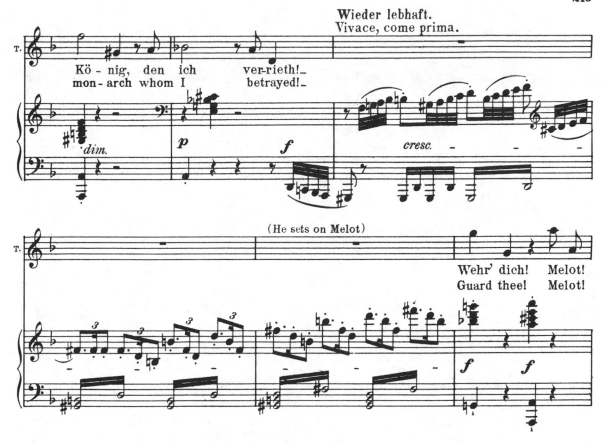

Kö - nig, den ich ver-rieth!_
mon-arch whom I betrayed!_

(He sets on Melot)

Wehr' dich! Melot!
Guard thee! Melot!

(As Melot thrusts his sword at him, Tristan lets his fall and sinks wounded into Kurvenal's arms; Isolda throws herself upon his breast. Mark holds back Melot. The Curtain falls quickly)

climactic point

Act III.

Scene I.

(The garden of a castle. At one side are high turrets, on the other a low breastwork broken by a watch-tower; at back the castle-gate. The situation is supposed to be on rocky cliffs; through openings one looks over a wide sea to the horizon. The whole scene gives an impression of being ownerless, badly kept, here and there delapidated and overgrown.

In the foreground inside lies Tristan sleeping on a couch, under the shade of a great lime-tree, extended as if lifeless. At his head sits Kurvenal, bending over him in grief, and anxiously listening to his breath-ing. From without comes the sound of a Shepherd's pipe)

(The Shepherd shows the upper half of his body over the breastwork, and looks in sympatheti-cally)

Shepherd.

(Kurvenal turns his head a little towards him)

Kurwe-nal! He! Sag', Kurwe-nal! Hör' doch, Freund! Wacht er noch nicht?
Kur-ve-nal! Ho! Say, Kur-ve-nal! Hear, my friend! Has he not waked?

Kurvenal. (He shakes his head sadly)

Erwachte er, wär's doch nur, um für im-mer zu ver-
And if he woke, it would be but to part from us for

schei - - den: er-schien zu-
ev - - er: un-less that

vor die Ärz-tin nicht, die einz' - - ge, die uns hilft.
doc-tress come, for she a-lone_____ can help us now.

Shepherd.

Sah'st du noch nichts? kein Schiff noch auf der See? Ei-ne and'-re
See'st nothing yet? no ship yet on the sea? Oh! a dif-f'rent

Wei - se hör - test du dann, so lustig als ich sie nur kann.
tune then pipe_ you I would, as mer-ry as ev-er I could.

Nun sag' auch ehr-lich, alter Freund: was hat's mit un-serm Herrn?
But tell me tru-ly, good my friend: what is it ails our lord?

Kurvenal.

Lass die Fra-ge: du kannst's doch nie er-fah-ren. Eif-rig
Leave the ques-tion: thou ne'er may'st know the an-swer. Watch ye

späh', und siehst du ein Schiff, so spie-le lu-stig und hell!
well; and sight ye a sail, pipe up then lust-y and loud!

K. Haus und Hof ge-pflegt, das einst mein Held zu Erb'und
kept the house and hall that once my lord to have and

K. Ei-gen an Leut' und Volk verschenkt, als Al-les er verliess, in frem-de Land' zu
hold to thy serfs and vas-sals gave, when all he left be-hind, to for-eign lands to

Tristan. Kurvenal.

K. zieh'n. In wel-ches Land? Hei! Nach
T. fare. What for-eign land? Aye! To
K.

Ein wenig breiter.
Poco più largamente.

K. Kornwall: kühn und won-nig, was sich da Glan-zes, Glückes und
Cornwall: where brave and happy, so much good for - tune, glo - ry and

K. Eh - - ren Tri-stan,mein Held,hehr er-trotzt!
hon - - our Tris - tan, my lord, no-bly won!

Etwas langsamer.
Poco più lento.
Tristan.
Kurvenal.
Tristan.

Bin ich in Kornwall? Nicht doch: in Ka-reoll *gedehnt* Wie kam ich
Am I in Cornwall? Ah! no! in Ka-reoll *steso* How came I

Etwas bewegter.
Poco più mosso.
Kurvenal.

her? Hei nun! Wie du kamst? Zu Ross rit-test du nicht; ein Schifflein führ-te dich
here? Eh now! How thou cam'st? A-horse camest thou not; a ship 'twas, car-ried thee

her: doch zu dem Schifflein hier auf den Schultern trug ich dich;
here: but to the ship, sire, 'twas on my shoulders bore I thee;

Etwas zurückhaltend.
Poco ritenuto.
Immer mehr belebend.
Sempre stringendo.

die sind breit: sie tru-gen dich dort zum Strand.
they are broad: they car-ried thee to the strand.

Nun bist
Now art

du da - heim, da - heim
thou at home, at home

zu Land: im
on land; thy

Etwas breiter.
Poco largamente.

ech - ten Land, im Hei - mathland; auf eig' - ner Weid' und
pro - per land, thy na - tive land; thine own are mead and

cresc.

immer
sempre

Won - ne, im Schein der al - ten Son - ne, dar -
mead - ow, in sun - shine and in shad - ow; when

Etwas zurückhaltend.
Poco ritenuto.

in von Tod und Wun - den du se - lig sollst ge - sun -
death and wounds are o - ver, where blithe - ly thou'lt re - cov -

dim.

sol - - - de, sü - - sse Hol - - de!
fair - - - est, sweet - - est, rar - - est!

Wann end - lich, wann, ach wann lö - schest du die
When, dear - est, when, ah! when wilt thou quench its

Immer ruhiger.
Sempre più tranquillo. (more and more faintly)

Zün - de, dass sie mein Glück mir kün - de?
burn - ing, that it may end my yearn - ing?

(He sinks back gently, exhausted.)

Das Licht, wann löscht es aus?
The light,— when dies that spark!

Wann wird es Ruh' im Haus?
When will the house be dark?

Mässig beginnend und schnell bewegter.
Moderato cominciando e poi stringendo subito.

Kurvenal (after great distress, quickly rousing himself from his dejection)

Der einst ich trotzt,' aus Treu' zu dir, mit dir nach ihr nun muss ich mich seh- - - nen.
For her who once, for faith to thee, was feared by me, with thee am I long- - - ing.

Glaub' meinem Wort: du sollst sie se-hen, hier und heut';
Take thou my word: for thou shalt see her, here, to-day:

den Trost_____ kann ich dir ge-ben,
That hope's_____ still in my giv-ing,

ist sie nur selbst noch am Le- - ben.
so she her-self still be liv- - ing.

heil - te leicht die Pla - - gen, von Me - lot's Wehr ge-
those could light - ly heal_ thee, that Me - lot's sword did

schla - gen. Die be - ste Ärz - - -
deal thee. Thy best phy - si - - -

ausdrucksvoll
espressivo

- - tin bald ich fand; nach Korn - wall
- - cian will she be; to Corn - wall

hab' ich aus - ge - sandt: ein treu -
has been sent by me a trust -

- er Mann wohl ü - ber's Meer bringt dir I - sol - den
- y man, who o'er the sea bring - eth I - sold' to

accel.

Gold!_____
gold!_____

cresc.

ff

poco riten.

a tempo

Musst' ich ver-ra-then den ed - len Herrn, wie be - trogst du ihn da so gern!
When I be-trayed him, my no - ble lord, then how will - ing was thine ac-cord!

poco riten.

a tempo

p

p

f

Noch beschleunigend.
Sempre stringendo.

Dir nicht__ ei-gen, ein - zig__ mein,
Thine thou__ art not, mine a - lone;

cresc.

più f

Sehr zurückhaltend.
Molto ritenuto.

Noch gedehnter.
Più allargando.

mit lei-dest du, wenn ich lei - de: nur was ich
thou suf-frest too, when I suf-fer: save, when I

ff espressivo e ben tenuto
ausdrucksvoll und sehr gehalten

Weniger gedehnt.
Meno largo.

lei - - de, das kannst du nicht
suf - - fer, then thou canst not

dim.

p

244

246 Mässig langsam.
Lento moderato.
(As Kurvenal hesitates to leave Tristan, who gazes at him in mute expectation, the mournful tune of the shepherd is heard, as at the beginning.)

(Cor anglais on the stage.)

Kurvenal (dejectedly)

Noch___ ist kein Schiff zu
Still___ there's no ship in

seh'n!
sight!

(Tristan has listened with waning excitement and now begins, with growing melancholy)

Tristan.

Muss ich dich so versteh'n, du al - te,
Must I so take thee, then, old tune so

ern‿ste Wei‿se, mit dei‿ner Kla‿ge Klang?
sad and sol‿emn, with all thy weight of woe?

Durch A‿ ‿ ‿bend‿
On eve‿ ‿ ‿ning

we‿ ‿hen drang sie bang, als einst dem Kind des
air ‿didst sad‿ ‿ly blow, to tell the child his

Va‿ ‿ ‿ters Tod ver‿kün‿ ‿det;‿
fa‿ ‿ ‿ther's death be‿fall‿ ‿en;

durch Mor‿ ‿gen‿grau‿en bang und
through morn‿ ‿ing's twi‿light, drear and

248

Sehr zurückhaltend.
Molto ritenuto.

bän-ger,   als der Sohn der Mut-ter Los _____ ver-nahm.
drear-er,   when the son his mother's fate _____ was told.

Etwas weniger zurückgehalten.
Poco meno ritenuto.

Erstes Zeitmass.
Tempo primo.

Da   er mich zeugt' und starb,   sie ster-bend mich ge-bar,
When he   who sired me died,   she died as I   was born.

die al - te Wei - se sehn- _____ -sucht - bang   zu
The old, old song to them, _____ as   well, brought

ih - nen wohl auch kla- - gend drang,   die einst mich
sor-row, too, and for- - tune fell,   that asked me

frug, und jetzt mich frägt: zu wel - chem Los   er - ko - ren, ich
then, and asks me now: What fate did life   al - lot me, when

Trank,   der der Qual mich ver-traut, ich selbst, ____
draught,   that my life has in-dued with pain, ____

Gedehnt.
Steso.

ich selbst, ____ ich hab' ihn ge-braut!
by me, ____ by me was it brew'd!

Aus Va- -ters Noth und Mut- -ter-Weh',
Of fa- -ther's grief, of moth- -er's cry,

aus Lie- bes-thrä-nen eh' und je, aus
of lov — ers' tears from aye and aye, from

Etwas drängender.
Poco più stringendo.

La-chen und Wei-nen, Won-nen und Wun-
joy and from wounds, ____ laugh-ter and sor-

es se - hen!
to see it!

Das Schiff?
The ship!

(Whilst Kurvenal, still hesitating, opposes Tristan,
the shepherd's pipe is heard without)

Säh'st du's noch nicht?___
See'st it not yet?___

trem.

(Cor anglais on the stage.)

p

Kurvenal (springing joyously up)

O Won - - - ne!
Thank heav - - - en!

pp

Sehr lebhaft.
Molto vivace.

Freu - - - - de!
Thank_____ heaven!

(Cor anglais on the stage.)

(He rushes to the watch-tower and looks out.)

Kurvenal (breathlessly)

Ha! das
Ha! the

Schiff! Von Nor-den seh'ich's na - - hen.
ship! From northward it is near - - ing.

Tristan.

Wusst' ich's nicht? Sagt' ich's nicht? dass sie noch lebt,
Knew I not? what said I! That she still lives,

noch Le - - ben mir webt? Die mir I - sol - - de
and life for me weaves! Naught but I - sold' the

ein - zig ent - hält, wie wär' I - sol - de mir aus der
world___ holds for me, how could I - sold' in my world not

Welt!
bel!

Kurvenal (shouting)

Hei - ha! Hei-ha!
A - hoy! A - hoy!

(Cor anglais on the stage.)

Wie es mu-thig steu-ert! Wie stark der Se - gel sich bläht! Wie es
see her brave-ly sail-ing! The sails, how fine - ly__ they draw! How she

(Orchestra)

Tristan.

jagt, wie es fliegt! Die Flag-ge? Die Flag-ge?
forg - es and flies! The pen-nant! The pen-nant!

Kurvenal.

Der Freu - - de Flag-ge am Wim-pel
The ga - - la flag's at the mast-head,

cresc. poco a

Scene II.

Sehr lebhaft.
Molto vivace.

(Kurvenal hastens away. — Tristan tosses on his couch in extreme excitement)

Tristan.

O_____ die-se Sonne!
O_____ sun that pourest!

Ha! dieser Tag! Ha dieser Won — ne son-nigster
Glo-rious ray! Joy thou re-stor — est, sun-ni-est

Tag! Ja — gendes Blut,___ jauch-zen-der
day! Cours-es my blood,___ grows my heart

Muth! Lust oh-ne Ma — ssen, freu —
good! Joy without mea — sure! Fren —

(He totters to the centre of the stage)

Isolda (without)

più f

ff trem.

dim.

Tri-
Tris-

-stan! Ge-lieb- -ter! Wie, hör' ich das Licht? die Leuch-te, ha!
-tan! Be-lov- -ed! What, hear I the light? the torch-light, ah!

Tristan (in frantic excitement)

Die Leuch - te ver-lischt! Zu ihr! Zu
The light is gone out! I come! To

f

p molto cresc.

Isolda hastens breathlessly in. Tristan, out of his senses, staggers weakly towards her.
They meet in the centre of the stage; she receives him in her arms)

ihr!
her!

ff sempre

Sehr allmählig nachlassend im Zeitmass. Poco a poco allargando.

ff

ff

Wun - - de, an der Wun-de stirb' mir nicht: uns Bei - den ver-
wounds, not of thewounds re - ceived in strife! For both, as if

Sehr zurückhaltend
Molto ritenuto.

eint er - lö - sche das Le - - - bens-licht!
one, ex - tin - guish the light_____ of life!

Gebrochen der Blick! Still das Herz!
All glassy his glance! Still his heart!

Nicht ei - nes A - - thems flücht'ges Weh'n!__
Hast not one fleet - - ing breath for me?__

(She sinks down senseless upon his body)

(Kurvenal had entered immediatly after Isolda; in speechless horror, he has remained near the entrance gazing motionless on Tristan. From below is now heard the dull tumult of voices and clash of weapons. The Shepherd climbs over the wall)

Lebhaft bewegt.
Allegro animato.

The Shepherd (coming quickly and softly to Kurvenal)

Kur-we-nal! Hör'!
Kur- ve-nal! Hear!

(Kurvenal starts up in haste and looks over the rampart, whilst the Shepherd stands apart gazing in consternation on Tristan and Isolda)

Ein zwei - tes Schiff!
An - oth - er ship!

Kurvenal.
Noch lebhafter.
Più vivo.
(angrily)

Tod und Höl-le!
Death's de-struction!

Al-les zur Hand!
Ready, my men!

Mar - ke und
Me - lot and

Me - lot hab' ich er-kannt.
Mark, they are to my ken!

Waffen und Steine!
Weapons and boulders!

Hilf mir! Ans Thor!
Help! to the gate!

(He hurries with the shepherd to the gate, which they hastily try to barricade)

The Helmsman (rushes in)

Mar - ke mir nach mit Mann und Volk: ver-geb'- ne Wehr, be -
Mark with his men are af - ter me: in vain we warred, for

Kurvenal.

wäl-tigt sind wir. Stell' dich, und hilf!
worsted are we! Stand by and help!

So lang' ich le - - - be, lugt mir Kei - ner her-
While life doth last, I let none en - ter a-

Brangæna.

I-sol - de! Her - rin! Glück und
I-sol - da! Mis - tress! Give you

Heil! Was seh' ich!
joy! What see I!

Immer noch beschleunigend.
Sempre più string.

(She devotes herself to Isolda)

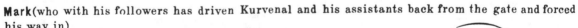

Ha! Lebst du, I - sol - de?
Ha! Liv'st thou, I - sol - da?

Mark (who with his followers has driven Kurvenal and his assistants back from the gate and forced his way in)

O Trug und Wahn! Tri -
O ly - ing dream! Tris -

Zurückhaltend.
Rallentando.
(Bending down sobbing over the bodies)

Jam——mer! Du treu-los___
sor——row! Thou faith-less,___

treu——ster Freund!
faith——ful friend!

Brangæna (who has revived Isolda in her arms)

Sie wacht, sie lebt! I-
She wakes, she lives! I-

Belebter.
Animando.

sol—de! hör' mich, vernimm mei-ne Süh-ne! Des Tran-kes Ge-
sol-da! hear me! Accept my a——tone-ment! The draught and its

heim-niss ent-deckt' ich dem Kö-nig: mit sor-gen-der
se-cret, I told the King of it: All anx-ious, with

Eil'stach er in See, dich zu er-rei-chen, dir__ zu ent-sa——gen, dir
speed he put to sea, that he might reach thee, so__ to re-nounce___ thee, and

Mässig bewegt.
Moderato con moto.
Mark.

B. M.

zu- zu- füh- — ren den Freund!
e'en so give— thee thy love.

War-
O

dolce

M.

um, I-sol- de, war- um mir das? Da hell mir ent-
why, I-sol- da, why this to me? When clear-ly I

M.

hüllt, was zu- vor ich nicht fassen konnt', wie se-lig, dass den Freund ich frei von
saw, what be- fore I had failed to grasp, how glad was I to find my friend from

M.

Belebend.
Animando.

Schuld da fand! Dem hol- den Mann — dich zu ver-
blame was free! Guilt-less was he; — so, to be-

M.

mäh- -len, mit vol- len Se- geln flog ich dir nach. Doch
troth ye, with flow-ing sails I flew af- ter thee. Too

Un-glü-ckes Un-ge-stüm, wie er-reicht es, wer Frie-den bringt? Die
wild is the course of woe, for the bring-er of joy t'o'er-take! Death's

ff *f* *p* *cresc.*

poco accel.

Ern-te mehrt' ich dem Tod. Der Wahn häuf- - -te die
har-vest I did but swell, fresh woe's er- - -ror com-

poco accel. *più f* *ff* *ff*

Allmählig zurückhaltend.
Rallentando poco a poco.

Brangæna.

(Isolda, unconscious of all around her, turns her eyes

Noth! Hörst du uns nicht? I-sol-de! Trau-te! Vernimmst du die Treu-e
pel! Hear'st thou us not? I-sol-da! Dearest! Mis-tak-est thou not the

p

Sehr mässig beginnend.
Molto moderato cominciare.
Isolda.

with rising inspiration on Tristan's body) *pp*

nicht? Mild und lei-se wie er lä-chelt,
truth? Fair and gently he is smiling;

pp *pp*